NOSTALGIC HAPPENINGS IN THE THREE BANDS OF JOHN PHILIP SOUSA

By
MALCOLM HESLIP

ISBN 0-918048-09-5

Library of Congress Catalog Card Number 82-81967

10 9 8 7 6 5 4 3

This book was originally created by Malcolm Heslip for two reasons.
First, to serve as a family keepsake and to preserve the memories of
his association with John Philip Sousa. Second, to provide gift copies to former members of Sousa's bands, Sousa enthusiasts, and
friends. Copies were also presented to 228 libraries. All 625 copies
of this gift book were produced privately in 1982 and 1983.

One recipient was the editor of Integrity Press, who regarded the
book as a highly entertaining work which recorded some rare history
in a unique way. He requested permission to publish it, thereby making it available to the public at large.

For this revised edition (1992), the design was changed slightly.
Except for minor updating and the addition of an index and extra
photographs, the contents are the same as the original. Also, acid-
free paper and a more durable library binding/cover combination
were used.

INTEGRITY PRESS   61 Massey Drive   Westerville, Ohio 43081

Manufactured in the United States of America

Dedicated to my wife
Doris Bice Heslip

JOHN PHILIP SOUSA

b. Washington, D.C.
   November 6, 1854

d. Reading, Pennsylvania
   March 6, 1932

CONTENTS

ILLUSTRATIONS

PREFACE

A series of twenty-five or more incidents—many of them participated in by the author—are described in this volume. It is being published in the sixtieth year after John Philip Sousa's death as a modest tribute from one who played as a young man under him in 1917 as a member of the United States Naval Training Station Band at Great Lakes, Illinois.

This distinguished bandmaster and composer led one of his three bands for a period of over half a century. He was appointed leader of the United States Marine Band in 1880. He formed his own professional touring concert band in 1892.

For the following thirty-nine years, this legendary band not only crisscrossed America regularly but made four extended tours of Europe. In addition, it made a year-long around-the-world tour.

In early 1917, Sousa suspended the operations of this civilian band and accepted a lieutenant's commission in the U.S. Naval Reserve. He was immediately placed in charge of the young musicians and the music program at the Great Lakes Naval Training Station. He developed a huge band there, as well as many small bands, which played in principal cities of America and provided bands for the fleet.

When released from the U.S. Navy in 1919, Sousa reinstituted his former professional civilian band. From that time on, audiences everywhere enthusiastically hailed his performances. During the remainder of his life, Sousa's Band continued to be the most popular of all the large musical organizations in the country.

Three generations of Sousas — John Philip Sousa, John Philip Sousa, Jr., and John Philip Sousa III. This photograph was apparently made the same day as the one shown on page 102 of the 1928 edition of Sousa's autobiography, *Marching Along*.

FOREWORD
By
John Philip Sousa IV

Some Thoughts about My Great-grandfather

The man who made my family name famous died sixteen years before I was born. His wife lived twelve years longer. Their son, my grandfather, John Philip Sousa, Junior, lived until I was eight. The third John Philip and his first wife Dorothy were my father and mother. One of my prized photographs (see illustration) is of the first three John Philip Sousas.

Members of my family and many others who personally recall my great-grandfather say that he was indeed an incredibly talented person who created and played music that stirred the patriotism of all who heard it.

Although I have known many who talked with my illustrious ancestor, I have met only a few who actually played in one of his bands.

I met Mr. Meredith Willson for a second time at the Washington, D.C., ceremony in 1976 at which John Philip Sousa was inducted into the Hall of Fame for Great Americans. The first time I met him was at the Elkhart, Indiana, Bicentennial Celebration which in part was put on by the Conn Instrument Corporation, maker of the first production Sousaphone. We had a very pleasant visit as he described some of his earlier experiences. By the time I met him, he was internationally known as the creator of *The Music Man* and other Broadway productions.

Twenty years ago, I met Dr. Malcolm Heslip, who played in Sousa's navy band at the Great Lakes Naval Training Station. Knowing I was a collector, he gave me photographs and mementos from his Sousa collection. In addition, he presented me with what must have been his cherished copy of *The Fifth String*, one of three novels written by Sousa. Also, the author told me about many incidents in connection with Sousa that are not included in this book. For instance, he often moved among the members of his naval band, picking up and examining the individual players' band instruments.

Many years later, I had the exciting experience of holding the author's musical instrument played in 1917 which my great-grandfather also held in his hands shortly after it was purchased.

Since the age of ten, I have been a collector and a fascinated student of things directly related to the days of Sousa. Most of you will, therefore, appreciate the feelings I had as I read this book. It comes as a welcome addition to the many things written about Sousa.

I am sure I speak for the other members of the Sousa family as I thank the author for his dedication and his devotion to the memory of John Philip Sousa.

June, 1992
Westlake Village, California

INTRODUCTION AND
ACKNOWLEDGMENTS

My earliest personal association with John Philip Sousa began in 1917. In that year, he suspended the operations of his famous professional civilian band and entered the United States Navy for active wartime duty.

Immediately, he took charge of the large and rather unwieldy band in which I had been a member for about one month. Actually, the band was a training school. It was designed to prepare young recruits with musicians' ratings to furnish shipboard music. It was my good fortune to remain under Sousa's direction for about seven months.

The friendly but determined bandmaster, from the very start, rehearsed the band almost relentlessly. It was the only way he could maintain anything approaching a professional level with a large band made up of an ever-changing group of members.

Within a short period, Sousa and this new naval band began to make appearances in support of various wartime activities. Over a period of a year and a half, he took this band to many of America's large cities.

Several of the following short stories cover events in Sousa's early life. These events occurred decades before I met him. They are based, for the most part, on things he wrote about himself. It should be noted that his friends knew him as a great storyteller. Perhaps, they said, facts were not always allowed to stand in the way of some of his stories.

In addition to Sousa's own writings, I have relied on the works of many authors. I wish to acknowledge my debt to each one of them. I am particularly indebted to Dr. Kenneth Berger for the materials in his book, *The March King and His Band*, and Mr. Paul E. Bierley for his biography, *John Philip Sousa, American Phenomenon*.

Most of Sousa's music manuscripts were not available for researchers until thirty-eight years after his death. Mr. Bierley was the first scholar to use these materials for a comprehensive study of this conductor and composer.

The remaining episodes in my series come from my own observations both while playing in Sousa's naval band and at other meetings that occurred intermittently in the 1920's in Chicago and Champaign, Illinois.

Mr. John Philip Sousa III favored me by giving permission to use many direct quotations that were copyrighted and published in *Marching Along* in 1928. I am also indebted to the *Saturday Evening Post* for permission to use certain quotations from Sousa's 1925 series of articles, *Keeping Time*.

In addition, I wish to thank Mr. John Philip Sousa IV for his interest and help in the preparation of this manuscript. He offered to share his collection of photographs, many of which are not in my scrapbook, of his great-grandfather's activities.

Others who gave me invaluable assistance after reading the manuscript are: Mrs. Eileen Fitch, Mr. George Waln, Mr. William Gould, my daughter Mrs. Susan McCormick, Mr. Don T. Hibbard, and my wife Doris.

Playing in one of Sousa's three large bands provided a heady experience for a young man just out of high school. Rehearsals, concerts, parades, and other ceremonies were filled with incidents a storyteller yearns for. Remembering what Sousa's friends said about his storytelling, I am not too sure about my own honesty as I recount the things that happened.

In no sense of the word should this book be considered a biography. Instead, it is the presentation of a series of nostalgic events that took place in the era of large touring concert bands.

CHAPTER 1
A UNITED STATES PRESIDENT'S
DEMAND

The President of the United States was speaking. "Sousa," he said, as he handed the bandmaster a piece of paper and called out the name of the song, "will you now play this dance?" The forty members of the Marine Band were playing at the White House. John Philip Sousa was their twenty-six year old leader.

"One of my guests," the President continued, "a professional dancer from Spain, will perform for us. She is now changing into her costume. Her act will end today's ceremony."

The startled bandmaster looked at the note in search of more information. The single word "Cachuca" was scribbled on it. The song was new to him. He tried to bluff by saying, "Sir, I am sorry, but we do not have this piece in our repertoire...."

"Why, Sousa, I thought you could play anything. I am sure you can. Now give us the 'Cachuca',"[1] interrupted the President. With this, he returned to his guests.

Most of the bandsmen were dismayed. However, one of the cornetists, a foreigner, rose quickly and said in an astonished voice, "I thought everyone in the world knew that song. In my country we sing it all of the time." He proceeded to play it softly for Sousa. Later, when Sousa wrote of the situation, he said, "I hastily wrote out several parts for the leading instruments and told the rest of the band to vamp."[2] Thus, for the moment, the piece was scored on the spot.

Then he gave explicit instructions as to how he wanted the piece played.

Minutes later, an official alerted the band that the dancer was ready to start. A presidential aid appeared with the beautiful performer. She was then presented to the President and his appreciative guests.

Following this, the dancer moved to the center of the floor,

---

1. Sousa, *Marching Along*, p. 80.
2. Ibid.

gave a signal to the bandleader, and the band burst forth confidently.

Her dance became an instant success. With the many repeats that were demanded, it provided a dazzling finale for President Chester A. Arthur's White House ceremony that day.

Some of the musicians carefully packed up their instruments and equipment and returned by streetcar to the Marine Barracks. Others, including the bandmaster, walked from there to their homes nearby.

A pleased Sousa related the details of the President's evening performance to his youthful bride, Jennie, who was spending her first year in Washington, D.C. Not unexpectedly, she expressed great pride in the resourcefulness displayed by her young husband in response to the insistent demand of the President.

John Philip's father, Antonio, was born in Spain of Portuguese parents who had fled Portugal. Antonio left Spain at an early age and came to the United States. Once in this country, he met and later married a girl, Maria Elisabeth Trinkaus, from Bavaria, who was visiting relatives in Brooklyn. The young Antonio and his bride soon moved to Washington, D.C. In those early days, he made his living as a musician.

John Philip, the third of ten children, was born to Elisabeth and Antonio on November 6, 1854. By the time the boy was three years old, Antonio had become a trombone player in the United States Marine Band. Within a few years, he was well aware that he had a musically talented son.

When John Philip was seven years old, Antonio enrolled his son in a conservatory. Two years later, Antonio was informed that not only did his son have perfect pitch, but he could read fairly difficult piano music on sight. Moreover, he could envision a score without having heard a note of it.

He attended this conservatory and studied violin during what turned out to be the four years of the Civil War.[3] In quick

3. Bierley, *John Philip Sousa, American Phenomenon*, pp. 23-28.

succession, the war ended, an assassin killed President Abraham Lincoln, and Andrew Johnson became President.

At first, the shock of President Lincoln's death was almost indescribable. Soon, however, those living in Washington, and those visiting the city, recovered enough to enjoy the huge parades of returning soldiers. Celebrations occurred for weeks. Martial music could be heard throughout the day. The young John Philip was tremendously impressed by both the parades and the music.

In his twelfth year, the energetic young violinist organized and directed his own seven-piece dance orchestra. It was made up of six grown men and himself. The following year, he became an apprentice musician in the United States Marine Band. Fortunately for the bandsmen, they were permitted to play in other musical organizations when off duty.

This enabled John Philip to be a first violinist in orchestras and to study harmony, composition, and violin under Mr. George Felix Benkert, one of the most talented music teachers and orchestra directors in Georgetown and Washington, D.C. Benkert, who directed a small symphony orchestra, employed John Philip to play first violin in the concerts the orchestra gave each month.

At the age of nineteen, the young violinist further distinguished himself when he became music director of a variety show on tour. Upon the conclusion of the tour, he decided to move to Philadelphia. At that time, he was determined to participate in the 1876 Philadelphia Centennial Celebration. This turned out to be an excellent move. His timing was perfect.

The manager of the official Centennial Orchestra immediately engaged Sousa to play in the first violin section. Jacques Offenbach, the famous French composer, conducted this orchestra.

During the years that elapsed before John Philip met Jennie, he continued to study harmony and composition and managed to publish some of his first pieces. Also, he did arranging for two Philadelphia music publishing houses, taught music, and played first violin—always his principal

Sousa was leader of the U.S. Marine Band from 1880 to 1892. He served under five Presidents of the United States: Hayes, Garfield, Arthur, Cleveland, and (Benjamin) Harrison.

activity—in theater orchestras. During this period, he completed his first operetta, *Katherine*.[4] Soon after completing it, the following coincidence took place.

4. Bierley, *The Works of John Philip Sousa*, p. 29.

CHAPTER 2
A BEAUTIFUL YOUNG UNDERSTUDY
MEETS THE MUSIC DIRECTOR

"Mr. Sousa," one of the soloists said, "this is Miss Jennie Bellis, a member of the cast. Today, for a special reason, we want her to meet the music director." Sousa turned to meet a stunningly beautiful girl.

"Well, good morning. This *is* a pleasure," responded the twenty-five year old violinist. Sousa wrote later:

> She had the most perfect complexion, I believe, of anybody on earth. She had on a little gray hat, sort of a poke bonnet effect, and was prettily dressed.
>
> After I had shaken hands with her, she said laughingly, "There are two birthdays today. I am celebrating Washington's and...."
>
> "And," I broke in, "Whose?"
>
> "Mine," she said. "I'm sixteen."[5]

They were rehearsing the new Gilbert and Sullivan operetta, *H.M.S. Pinafore*. Its tuneful melodies were being presented to the American public this year for the first time.

"I am really only an understudy," Jennie remarked. Then she added in a slightly excited voice, "Isn't this a wonderful operetta? Philadelphia theatergoers are certainly going to be captivated by your arrangement of it. Under your direction our rehearsals are musical adventures."

Sousa said later that this was no ordinary introduction. He arranged for them to spend an evening together as soon as possible. They continued to see each other as time permitted.

Under Sousa's direction, *Pinafore* was performed several times in Philadelphia and then went on tour, playing seven weeks on Broadway in New York City.[6]

---

5. Sousa, *Marching Along*, pp. 62-63.
6. The troupe, originally an amateur organization, was called the Amateur Opera Company. It gradually became professional and was eventually known as Gorman's Original Church Choir "Pinafore" Company.

"...A cloud of chestnut hair...a perfect complexion...quite the loveliest little girl I had ever seen...." That was Sousa's first impression of the Philadelphia girl, Jane Van Middlesworth Bellis, who became his wife in 1879.

Soon John Philip and the sixteen[7] year-old Jennie became engaged. They were married on December 30, 1879, fully expecting to make their home in Philadelphia. Less than a year later, however, they left that city and moved to Washington. D.C.

7. The actual age of Jane Van Middlesworth Bellis Sousa has not been definitely established. Her birthdate is not the same on all documents. After her death in 1944, her two daughters could not agree on the birthdate.

CHAPTER 3
A MARINE AND A "MARCH KING"

The first hint of their move from Philadelphia came in September, 1880, when Sousa, again on tour, received a letter while in St. Louis. That letter contained an offer for him to become leader of the United States Marine Band. Sousa's father, although retired from the band, had helped negotiate the offer.

The young orchestra director accepted the position. It placed him in charge of the "President's Own Band," the only musical organization to play for White House functions. In the years that followed, Sousa and the Marine Band played hundreds of public weekly concerts at the White House, the Marine Barracks, and on the steps of the Capitol Building.

As leader of this band, Sousa established a national reputation for both himself and the band. He served with distinction under Presidents Rutherford B. Hayes, James A. Garfield, Chester A. Arthur, Grover Cleveland, and Benjamin Harrison.

The Columbia Phonograph Company engaged Sousa's Marine Band to make some of the earliest recordings for the newly-invented phonograph. Sousa did not conduct for the recordings, however.

Three Sousa children were born in Washington, D.C., beginning with John Philip, Jr. in 1881, followed by Jane Priscilla in 1882, and Helen in 1887. The nearly twelve years spent in that city provided an exciting time for the entire family.

While walking in downtown Washington after he became a well known person, Sousa was stopped by one of Washington's prominent officials.

The *Washington Post* newspaper official said, "Over twenty thousand school children and parents will gather at the Smithsonian grounds Saturday. They will be there not only to hear your Marine Band concert but to get the names of the winners of my newspaper's Prize Essay Contest."

"Yes," answered Sousa, "It will be a big day."

9

During the twelve-year period in which Sousa directed the U.S. Marine Band, the band came to be regarded as America's finest military band and was referred to as "the government band." This photograph was taken in Cape May, New Jersey, in 1891.

"Is it asking too much to request that you compose a special piece for the event?" asked the official. "My newspaper will give it wide publicity and play up the fact that it will be the premiere performance of the piece."

"It would be difficult to produce a complete piece in three days," came the answer.

"Not for a young musical genius like you, who has the reputation of creating music at a faster rate than that," responded the official.

"Of course I can do it, but it may not turn out to be one of my best pieces," he replied.

Nevertheless, the young composer produced the piece on schedule. Wisely, he named it the *Washington Post*. Over twenty-five thousand individuals did show up that Saturday in 1889. They enthusiastically applauded the first public playing of this number.

Many years later, when Sousa wrote about creating the *Washington Post* march, he said:

> It was chosen almost immediately by the dancing masters at their yearly convention to introduce their new dance, the two-step. I sold this famous tune to a Philadelphia publisher for thirty-five dollars.[8]

In his lifetime, Sousa would compose some 137 marches. Perhaps all Sousa researchers and enthusiasts now place *Washington Post*, produced in these three days, in the top six of this long list of his marches.

A century later, bands throughout the world keep this piece in their repertoire and play it regularly.

8. Sousa, *Marching Along*, pp. 115-117.

CHAPTER 4
SOUSA FORMS HIS OWN BAND

Under the leadership of the talented and resourceful Sousa, the United States Marine Band became the finest military music organization in the country. Nevertheless, the bandmaster was not promoted to commissioned officer rank.

Moreover, at the age of thirty-seven, he indicated to friends that he hoped sometime to lead a civilian band of his own. This aspiration, combined with his disappointment in not being promoted, made him receptive to a splendid offer.

For many years, the popular Patrick S. Gilmore had conducted the finest civilian band in the United States. One of his former managers, Mr. David Blakely, became aware of Sousa's accomplishments. This experienced tour director proposed that Sousa resign and form a civilian band. Blakely would organize a company to finance and manage it. The leader would be paid four times his salary at the time.

Understandably, Sousa resigned and immediately formed a touring concert band under this arrangement. The band's first performance took place on September 26, 1892, in Plainfield, New Jersey. Two days before this concert, however, a shocking event occurred. The well-liked and firmly established bandmaster Patrick Gilmore died. In a matter of weeks, it became apparent that Gilmore's group would not enjoy great success under another leader.

Under the circumstances, Sousa proceeded to employ over a dozen musicians from this group. Herbert L. Clarke, who was later to be regarded as the greatest cornetist of all time, became one of those musicians, as did Arthur Pryor, a trombonist of equal stature. Sousa also took over the contract of the former Gilmore organization to play for the 1893 Chicago World's Fair. From that time on, nothing could stop the progress of Sousa and his new organization.

In the next seven years, the band played at all important fairs and expositions in the United States. Then in 1900, the musicians made their first tour of Europe. While there, among many other activities, they represented the United States at the

Paris [International] Exposition.

Returning home, Sousa and the band continued to give their regular annual concerts in virtually every section of the country. Moreover, they made three additional successful trips to Europe. These were made in 1901, 1903, and 1905. In the meantime, Sousa produced a steady stream of very popular marches as well as several successful operettas.

In his *History of American Music*, published in 1904, Louis C. Elston wrote that John Philip Sousa had more performances of his works in France, Germany, and England than all of the other musicians included in his book.[9]

Then, in 1910-1911, the band went on its highly publicized year-long around-the-world tour. On this tour, Sousa and the band reached the climax of almost two decades of highly successful performances. Upon returning to the United States, their popularity continued. For example, between 1911 and 1914, the average weekly attendance of the New York concerts was 60,000 persons.[10]

These exciting events took place in an era of large touring concert bands. The creative musician, Sousa, firmly established himself as the "American Phenomenon" so aptly described in Paul Bierley's delightful 293-page biography of Sousa published in 1973 [revised in 1986].

As might be expected, when a bandmaster conducts his concerts all over the world decade after decade, events do not always take place as planned. Accidents will happen. Baggage will get lost. Mistakes sometimes occur. Also, humorous situations develop. On occasion, even an attempt is made to hoodwink the conductor.

9. Elston, p. 154.
10. Berger, *The March King and His Band*, p. 25.

This is the first known group photograph of Sousa's civilian band, taken in St. Louis in 1893. At that time, the band's uniforms resembled those of the U.S. Marine Band. The uniforms were changed to navy blue for a short period and were thereafter solid black.

CHAPTER 5
BEING SPOOFED AND LIKING IT

"Has anyone ever heard of the *Monongahela Waltz*?" Sousa looked at the pile of several thousand postal cards on the table and continued, "It has received about one hundred times more votes for the contest than its nearest competitor." Not a single bandsman could recall it.

They were counting the postal card nominations for numbers to be played at the Pittsburgh Composer's Contest.

A secretary wrote the composer of the waltz requesting that he bring in his band arrangement.

Three days before the contest, a personable young man appeared and identified himself as the composer of the *Monongahala Waltz*. He carried the music in an envelope.

A quick glance established it as a completely acceptable entry. Unbelievably, however, all of the music appeared on one piece of paper.

The astonished bandmaster asked the young composer to explain how sixty-five members of the band could read from one sheet of music. Contestants were required to provide the band with fully scored entries, plus parts for the band to play at the contest.

At first the man appeared puzzled but recovered instantly when Sousa demanded, "With only this one page in existence, how did hundreds of individuals know about your creation?"

Many years later, when Sousa wrote about this incident in his autobiography, he said:

> I finally extracted from him the information that he had bought ten dollars worth of postcards and had asked his friends and acquaintances to send in requests for the piece, hoping I would arrange it for my band. I did.[11]

---

11. Sousa, *Marching Along*, pp. 242-243.

Sousa was sometimes criticized by his managers for inserting new music at concerts on the spur of the moment. He was a champion of American music and performed many unfamiliar works for the benefit of lesser known contemporaries.

CHAPTER 6
"ONE OF THE MOST VIVID INCIDENTS IN MY CAREER"

"Perhaps you should be putting the melody down on paper."
His wife had said this to Sousa as the two paced the deck of the
passenger ship *Teutonic* the second day out of Naples, Italy.
"As distressed as you are, some of it may escape you."

"It will not get away from me," he replied.

Only five days earlier, the Sousas were vacationing in
Europe. While there, they were informed of the death in New
York City of David Blakely, the manager of the band. They
were now returning to the United States to face a series of stag-
gering problems.

Sousa would be required personally to manage the upcom-
ing twenty-week tour. The bandmaster wrote later that, on this
ship and in this mood, there occurred one of the most vivid
incidents of his career.

In describing the extraordinary events of the next ten days,
Sousa said:

> Suddenly, I began to sense the rhythmic beat of a band
> playing within my brain. It kept on ceaselessly, playing,
> playing, playing. Throughout the whole tense voyage,
> that imaginary band continued to unfold the same
> themes, echoing and re-echoing the most distinct mel-
> ody. I did not transfer a note of that music to paper while
> I was on the steamer, but when we reached shore, I set
> down the measures that my brain-band had been playing
> for me, and and not a note of it has ever been changed.[12]

Sousa named the piece *The Stars and Stripes Forever.* It
became, as most everyone knows, his most popular march.

Photocopies of the music he placed on paper on Christmas
Day of 1896 are owned and cherished by thousands of Sousa
enthusiasts. His band played this piece at least once in every

12. Sousa, *Marching Along*, p. 157.

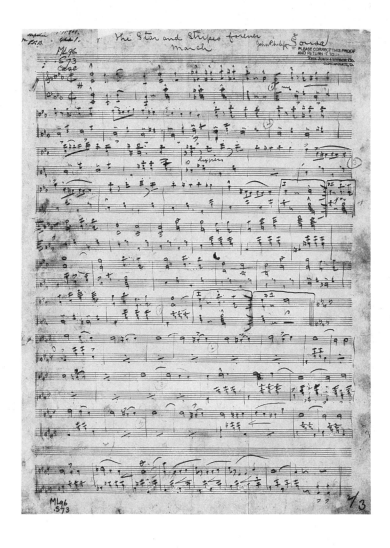

The first sketch of *The Stars and Stripes Forever* was made on Christmas Day, 1896. Although many thought it was the official national march

of the United States of America, it was not so designated until ninety
years later.

concert he directed in the following thirty-five years. Many times, at the demand of an audience, the number had to be played several times in a single concert.

During the sixty-year period that has elapsed since his death in March of 1932, bands all over the world continue to play *The Stars and Stripes Forever* regularly for every possible kind of occasion. By any measure, it has been the most popular and durable march ever written, and in 1987 it was designated the official national march of the United States.

CHAPTER 7
KING EDWARD VII
PRESENTS MEDAL TO SOUSA

Presentation of the Medal of the Victorian Order to Sousa took place a few minutes after a command performance at Sandringham. England's King Edward VII arranged for the concert as a surprise for his Queen Alexandra's birthday. The King's mother, Queen Victoria, had died only eleven months earlier.

On that December day in 1901, the band made the four-hour trip from London to the railroad station near Sandringham. Sousa, his wife and two daughters, rode in the King's automobile from there to the castle. Royal carriages transported the band members.[13]

The printed program for the concert showed thirteen selections. It was warmly received by the twenty distinguished persons who attended the performance.

As the Sousas and the King and Queen engaged in a friendly visit after the concert, the medallion was presented. With a few appropriate remarks, the King personally handed the medal to Sousa. It was enclosed in a beautiful box. The Prince of Wales, however, would add something to the amenities of the delightful occasion.

During the evening, the King praised both Sousa's music and his musical organization. Also, he expressed great admiration for his compositions. When Sousa wrote about the event, he said:

> The Queen remarked graciously on Mrs. Sousa's
> unusual beauty and the Prince of Wales took the casket
> from my hand, drew out the medal and said, amiably,
> "Where shall I pin it, Mr. Sousa?"

13. Lingg, *John Philip Sousa*, pp. 160-161. The author writes that Mrs. Sousa engaged a Parisian designer in London to make a dress for the occasion. When it was delivered, however, Sousa decided that the all ice-blue taffeta was too cold a color and selected, instead, a gown of white silk that was dotted with pink roses. They had brought this with them from the United States.

Sousa's Band was credited with having created more goodwill abroad than a whole corps of diplomats. The band made tours of Europe in 1900, 1901, 1903, and 1905 and finally a tour around the world in 1910-1911. It is shown here with the Grenadier Guards Band of England in 1901.

"Over my heart," I replied.

"How American!" he smiled.[14]

After the presentation of the medal, Sousa asked for permission to compose a march and dedicate it to the King.

Two years later, Sousa and the band performed a second concert for the King and Queen. This time it occurred at Windsor Castle. Long before this meeting, however, Sousa had created the *Imperial Edward* march.[15] Sousa did not regard this as one of his better marches, but it is still performed in America and abroad.

14. Sousa, *Keeping Time*, Part 5 (December, 1925), p. 163.
15. Bierley, *The Works of John Philip Sousa*, pp. 62-63.

CHAPTER 8
A SUPERLATIVE PERFORMANCE
AT WARWICK CASTLE

"Will you arrange for the Sousa Band to give a concert for me at Warwick Castle?" asked the Countess of Warwick. The question, asked at the start of the 1903 European tour, was directed to the manager of the band's concerts in England. The request had all of the overtones of a command.

Within a few days, the band would give a matinee in Stratford-on-Avon and a night concert in Leamington. Both locations were in the general vicinity of Warwick Castle.

"All of the band members," Sousa's manager answered, "would be very happy to visit and perform in your famous castle. It is a great compliment to a foreign band. I am truly sorry, however, to have to say that it is booked solidly for the remainder of its stay in England."

Although he was conscious of the lady's wealth and social position, he had not heard about her reputation of being resourceful in getting her own way. Momentarily, the manager thought the matter was closed.

"Well," persisted the lady, "you are to play in Leamington on the eighteenth. Why not play for me after the Leamington concert? Give me a midnight concert, and I will announce the hour to my guests."[16]

When consulted, Sousa readily agreed. Band members were always paid extra for these special concerts. Also they would, no doubt, enjoy seeing the castle. The manager proceeded with arrangements for the affair, with the Countess agreeing to supply a sufficient number of conveyances to transport the band and all of its equipment and trunks of music from Leamington to Warwick Castle.

On the night of the performance, however, the caravan encountered some of the worst weather of the year.

The pleased host and hostess, the Earl, and the Countess, went out of their way to make the occasion a never-to-be-for-

16. Sousa, *Marching Along*, p. 234.

gotten party for the musicians and about forty guests invited to share the midnight performance.

It became something more than an outstanding concert. The musicians were justifiably proud of what they achieved. All of the conveyances in the trip from Leamington that stormy night succeeded in arriving before the concert except the one bringing the trunks of music. It had a bad accident and reached the castle after the concert had been completed.

The warmly received and superbly played concert was played entirely from memory.

Sousa's *Yorktown Centennial* march, dated 1881, was written to commemorate the 100th anniversary of the Revolutionary War at Yorktown, Virginia. The march had a short-lived second title; the Sen Sen Chiclet Company issued a piano version in 1901, renaming it *Sen Sen*.

CHAPTER 9
AN UNLUCKY DAY IN
MANNHEIM, GERMANY

"No doubt you are Herr Sousa?" The English-speaking newspaper reporter confronted the bandmaster as he emerged from the train station in Mannheim, Germany.

"Indeed I am," he responded jovially.

"But why are you arriving in our city without the members of your band?"

"I left Paris last night two hours ahead of them. Their three cars are attached to a later train which will arrive in plenty of time for our concert tonight," the bandmaster answered confidently. As everyone knows, however, European railroad officials are capable of all kinds of mischief.

Unknown to the manager and members of the band, train officials detached two of their cars from the train at midnight. The two cars were attached to trains going to two different destinations.

One contained all of the medium-sized and large instruments and trunks. The other "accommodated" one half the sleeping musicians.

The car that remained attached to the train arrived in Mannheim on schedule. One of the lost cars showed up an hour before concert time, while the baggage car with the music and all but the small hand-carried cases of instruments never did reach Mannheim. (Fortunately for the band members, it arrived in Heidelberg the next day in time for a highly successful concert in that city.)

The impatient audience, well aware of the situation, was asked to wait an extra hour. Then, as Sousa admitted defeat, the affair was canceled and refunds were made.

Later, when Sousa wrote of the sorry circumstances, he said:

> I made the announcement through an interpreter to the audience, assuring them that they were the artistic center of the universe and I hoped I could return later and give

27

them a concert.[17]

The sentiment expressed in the announcement did not in the least impress the manager of the theater. He insisted on being paid damages for non-appearance. When an agreement could not be reached as to the actual amount, he took the problem to the local magistrate.

As a result, Sousa was required to pay the theater manager $1,200 before he was allowed to leave the beautiful German city of Mannheim.

17. Sousa, *Marching Along*, pp. 207-209.

CHAPTER 10
NOT THE WAY TO TREAT
A VISITING BANDMASTER

It happened in Wales during a concert at the Drill Hall in Merthyr Tydfil. The existing stage could not accommodate the entire band. Days before the concert, the theater manager employed workmen to extend the floor out over the orchestra pit.

Twenty-two of the fifty-five players and Sousa started the performance on this extended section.

While playing *The Fairest of the Fair*, the director motioned for the six trombone players sitting in the back row to come to the front. They did this.

As they added their weight to the new construction, one half of it collapsed. Sousa, music stand and all, plunged through the temporary platform and disappeared from sight.

The sounds created by the splintering lumber and crashing furniture were accompanied by screams from the startled audience.

Sousa never forgot this experience. He said of it:

> It is a breath-snatching sensation to fall seven feet below the floor with nothing to catch onto. I went down in a cloud of dust and debris and the prima donna, Miss Root, on hearing the crash, believed I had been killed and rushed out on the stage, screaming. I quickly righted myself, however, crawled up from the depths, bowed to the audience, and said, "We will now continue." Calmly we finished the programme.[18]

During the remainder of the program, however, the audience observed a novel seating arrangement. Since only one-half of the "new construction" had crashed, Sousa and forty-four members performed from the stage floor level. The other eleven musicians played from the level of the orchestra

18. Sousa, *Marching Along*, p. 265.

Courtesy Barry Owen Furrer

This 1903 photograph, made while on tour in England, is one of the few existing photographs of Sousa's Band in concert formation. Not all stages were this substantial; one collapsed two years earlier in Wales, but Sousa and his musicians miraculously escaped serious injury.

pit floor seven feet below and to the left of the conductor.

Not surprisingly, the audience actually cheered Sousa and the other musicians at the end of each selection played during the "second half" of the performance.[19]

19. The stage collapse is described in a diary kept by Albert Knecht, saxophone player in the band at the time. As an interesting sidelight, Knecht noted that the contractor who built the stage was also an undertaker.

CHAPTER 11
UPSTAGING THE UNITED STATES CONSUL IN GERMANY

"Mr. Sousa, please do not expect a responsive audience tonight," said the United States Consul. The Sousas were dining with the consul and his wife two hours before the first of three concerts to be given in Hanover, Germany. This meeting took place just after the turn of the century.

"The German people are much more interested in our agricultural products and other commodities," the consul continued, "than they are in our cultural activities."

Sousa pointed out that the band had already performed successfully in many European cities, including Paris, Berlin, and Brussels. He expected to get the same response in Hanover.

The somewhat opinionated, although not unfriendly, consul could not have been more mistaken.

Not only did the audience enthusiastically applaud the regularly scheduled numbers, it took advantage of the famous composer's generosity. It made him play encore after encore until the normal length of the concert was extended for over an hour.

It was past midnight when the consul and his wife and the Sousas left the concert hall. An impromptu reception had taken place in the corridor near the consul's box. Scores of friends and other theatergoers had formed a line and insisted on being introduced to Sousa. The consul was overjoyed.

Mrs. Sousa, who had been joined by their daughters Helen and Priscilla, retired to their hotel room. Still elated, the consul insisted that the remaining three go to his home and pick up a bottle of Kentucky bourbon. They then returned to a private room in the hotel's cafe, whereupon they celebrated Sousa's fantastic success.

The consul's wife, who did not care to drink that night, promptly curled up on a couch and went to sleep. This left the two men free to toast anyone they could think of. Emptying the bottle, and the further consumption of other drinks ordered from the hotel's bar, coincided with the arrival of dawn.

Thus, Sousa went to his room at daybreak. Never a heavy drinker, he sat on the edge of his bed for a short time until the awesome fact dawned on him that he had to direct a 2:30 p.m. and a 7:30 concert that day. Describing the predicament facing him, Sousa said that his mind was clear enough to realize that extraordinary measures were required to meet the needs of the day.

He called to his room the waiter who had been serving him. After a short conversation, he instructed him to bring up four quart jugs of Seltzer water.

In the next few hours, he slowly absorbed these four quarts into his digestive system. This, he felt, would prevent any additional alcohol from entering his bloodstream. The fact that he was a man in splendid physical condition may also have helped him face his crisis. He resisted the idea of lying down.

Following a light lunch at one o'clock, he appeared on the stage as scheduled at two-thirty. Although there was nothing easy about it, he caused his band to perform in a manner that produced sensational responses from a delighted audience.

That night, Sousa faced an even more enthusiastic audience. Individuals called for encores by name. All requests were for pieces composed by Sousa. Again, the concert ended much later than expected.

After the concert, as previously arranged, the Sousas met their two friends at the hotel dining room. It was revealed that the consul had been in bed all day. It was difficult for him to believe that the bandmaster had conducted his scheduled concerts that day.

In the meantime, Hanover officials and friends came to the table and congratulated the bandmaster on his spectacular performance. The baffled consul looked at the exhilarated Sousa, who had not slept for almost forty hours, and said, "Then our drinking bout did not even trouble you?"

Not surprisingly, the exuberant Sousa put on an act. He

looked at the haggard consul and, as he related later, said impressively: "Consul, you have been here twelve years. You have grown soft. Go back to America, my dear sir, and be a man again."[20]

The following day, Sousa, his wife, and two daughters and the band proceeded to their next engagement, in Halle. In all of the remaining cities of the European tour, Sousa and his band were hailed by enthusiastic audiences in much the same manner as in Paris, Berlin, Brussels, and Hanover.

20. Sousa, *Marching Along*, pp. 204-207.

CHAPTER 12
A STAR-STRUCK REPORTER URGES SOUSA TO START AUTOBIOGRAPHY

"I managed," said the reporter, "to hear twelve of the concerts you played during your ten-week engagement here at the Exposition." The Panama-Pacific International Exposition was ending that day. Sousa planned to leave San Francisco the following day to complete the 1915 annual tour. A slightly star-struck reporter was completing the last of several interesting and meaningful interviews with the bandmaster.

The band played concerts all the way from New York to the west coast before stopping in San Francisco for this very successful engagement.

"Surely no other city has received you in as friendly a manner as has San Francisco," remarked the reporter. The bandmaster gave an affirmative nod. With this, the reporter thought the interview was ended.

Sousa, however, seemed in no hurry. Apparently sensing this, the reporter casually asked, "Are you keeping a personal diary of all these exciting happenings, Mr. Sousa?"

"Not exactly," he replied, "but I do make all kinds of notes in the band's press books."

"When are you planning to share these fabulous experiences with your admiring public?" he was asked.

"As you know," Sousa replied, "I am now over sixty. Perhaps in another ten years I will take time off to write [a book] of my experiences."

"The musical highlights of your career will make a fascinating book. It is too bad that we must wait that long for it."

"Musical highlights!" remarked Sousa, "That is a splendid idea. It might be the best approach to a story of my life. Beginning in 1880, when I became leader of the Marine Band, a series of historically interesting musical events began to happen. Three of my most enduring marches were published, and my first operetta was produced.

"Later, in 1892, the act of forming my own civilian band was undoubtedly my most important musical milestone. My greatest march was created in 1896. Fifteen years ago, in 1900, we made our first European tour. You filed many stories about it. Every country in which we played provided highlights.

"Scores of enterprises in the United States, such as the St. Louis World's Fair and, later the Corn Palace Exposition in South Dakota, the Pittsburgh Exposition and many others provided significant events and musical episodes which could be included."

Sousa continued this nostalgic conversation with the reporter, "I can recall many incidents that occurred on the 1901, 1903, and 1905 European trips. Also, your own newspaper articles, five years ago in 1910, included many important musical events about us during the year we were on our world tour. Mrs. Sousa and our daughters Priscilla and Helen, who went with us, were included in some of the events you wrote about."

"My interview with you in 1911," the reporter said, "was an unusual one. In fact, as you may recall, it was not actually an interview. The *Los Angeles Times* had asked you to write this one yourself. You dictated it to your secretary on your way from San Bernardino to Los Angeles. He proceeded to type it on a typewriter in the Alexandria Hotel before you and your band went to Long Beach for the evening's concert.

"You had just returned from your around-the-world tour and were finishing the North American segment of concerts before starting eastward. Later, you ended the year-long tour with a big concert at the New York Hippodrome.

"I will always remember the size of some of the European audiences that your written 'interview' mentioned. After playing a four-week engagement at the Glasgow International Exhibition, you said that the actual turnstile count of the attendance, on the night of the final concert, was over 153,000. With performances and engagements like this, it is no wonder that you have received decorations and awards from the heads of foreign countries.

"By the way, when you write your 'musical highlights'

story, I hope you will describe these medals and tell us some individual stories about the actual presentations."

"They should, of course, be mentioned," he replied. "The awards you are referring to mean very little to me. Essentially, I am an entertainer. My greatest pleasure and stimulation comes from playing for the thousands of audiences in the United States and other countries throughout the world.

"It may seem strange to you, but I enjoy being received year after year by the same audiences. Our many appearances here in San Francisco, for instance, are always exciting events. The same thing is true for our repetitive engagements at Manhattan Beach, New York, and Willow Grove Park in Philadelphia."

The interview again appeared to be ending. The reporter, however, asked one more question. It came almost as an afterthought.

"What are some of your plans for the band, Mr. Sousa?"

"At present, I see no change in the plans made for the next few years. The war in Europe obviously precludes all foreign tours for us for possibly many years.

"Now that the Exposition is ending, we will begin our tour eastward in which we cross the entire United States. We will play in scores of large and small cities. When this schedule is ending, we will go to Philadelphia's Willow Grove Park for one month. This will be followed by an engagement of two weeks at the Pittsburgh Exposition. After this has been completed, we will go to New York City to open the extravaganza, *Hip Hip Hooray,* at the Hippodrome. Charles Dillingham has engaged us to play the next two winter seasons there. The first season will start in September and end in May, 1916. The other starts a little later and ends in May, 1917.

"In the unlikely event that the United States is drawn into the European war, I am sure that I would again volunteer my services just as I did in 1898."

There were other points of view about the United States becoming involved. The European war had been in progress for almost a year. Only two months before this interview, the

Mrs. John Philip Sousa (this photo ca. 1915), her son, and two daughters seldom traveled with the band. They sometimes attended concerts, however, when the band had a lengthy engagement in one location. They would often be escorted to the stage to be introduced just before an intermission. It was usually Priscilla, the older daughter who never married, who accompanied her mother. Mrs. Sousa was a retiring person and preferred to stay in the background.

British Cunard passenger ship *Lusitania* was sunk by a German submarine. It went down in an hour after it was hit. Almost one thousand lives were lost, including more than two hundred Americans.[21]

Many persons in the United States were already in doubt as to whether a policy of neutrality could be maintained in view of the circumstances that might have to be faced.

21. Charles Klein, librettist of two of Sousa's operettas, was one of those who perished when the *Lusitania* was sunk on May 15, 1915.

CHAPTER 13
NAVY RECRUITS MEET
THE "MARCH KING"

"You are about to share an important moment with me." Sousa made this statement at a morning rehearsal in 1917. More than two years had elapsed since his interview with the reporter discussed in the preceding chapter. He would soon be sixty-three years of age.

Seconds earlier, the writer and about 150 other young men stood at attention as Sousa entered the rehearsal room. They watched him walk briskly to the podium. In response to his cheerful "Good Morning," they relaxed and resumed their seats. The scene had occurred scores of times in the past few months.

Most of these men were former members of youth or town bands. Only a few had been employed previously as full-time musicians. Most of them had enlisted in the U.S. Navy for sea-duty assignments shortly after President Woodrow Wilson asked Congress for a declaration of war in April.

Long before this rehearsal took place, the young men read an almost unbelievable article in the newspapers. It said that engagements of the famous Sousa Band were suspended for the duration of the war.

Sousa was to become a Naval Reserve lieutenant and be assigned to their Naval Training Center at Great Lakes, Illinois. The newspapers reported that he would immediately be placed in charge of all musician recruits.

Within days, Sousa appeared in civilian attire on the reviewing stand with Captain William A. Moffett. Another person, quickly recognized as Herbert L. Clarke, the great cornetist, was a third reviewer. The remaining guest was identified later by the Training Center's magazine as the famous composer John Alden Carpenter from Chicago. Initially, he had persuaded Sousa, his close personal friend, to assist Captain Moffett with the development of the Center's bands.

After no more than a half hour of playing and marching, the Commandant ended the affair and returned to the Administration Building. This left Sousa and Clarke free to get acquainted with the bandsmen. It was a pleasant occasion. The cornetists could not believe they were unexpectedly in the presence of Herbert L. Clarke. As he visited with many small groups, he examined and played many of the cornets.

During the next hour, Sousa visited easily with dozens of the young musicians about the actual instruments they held in their hands, where they were from, and what their aspirations were. Finally the two guests returned to the Administration Building for lunch and another conference with Captain Moffett. The band members went to their quarters convinced they were now members of a Sousa musical organization.

Weeks later, the distinguished bandmaster arrived at the station in uniform. Officers and bandsmen gave him an outdoor reception. It was a cold and windy day. Sousa wore his overcoat. Several officers wore their boat capes (see photograph). All of those who visited with him must have been impressed by the bandmaster's friendliness and his modesty. Above all, they were surprised at his incredible optimism. He insisted that rehearsals start the next day.

Now, many rehearsals later, Sousa was sharing a special moment with members of his band.

"We are going to play my newest piece," he announced. "It is a march. Since I do not use a piano or any other musical instrument when I am producing my music, no one has ever heard a note of it."

Then holding the sheets of music high, he said, "Today we will read from handwritten manuscript. Remember, your ears will be the first to hear the strains of this new composition. Take a few minutes to study the music. Until we actually play it, however, do not make a single sound on any band instrument." Assistants quickly handed the music to the various sections heads.

In about five minutes, Sousa resumed his place on the podium. His friendly and easygoing manner had changed.

He became almost a martinet as he said, "You are to give me your best effort." It was a command. "Under no circum-

41

An outdoor reception was given for Lieutenant John Philip Sousa at the Great Lakes Naval Training Station on his first day of active duty in 1917. This snapshot was made by the author.

stances," he continued, "will we stop before the piece is completed. I must hear it in its entirety."

The excited young musicians were going to participate in a once-in-a-lifetime adventure with a great musician. Certainly they would give him their best.

Suddenly they heard themselves playing a stirring military march. The conductor, not surprisingly, became completely absorbed in the music.

The strains they were hearing were from the soon-to-be-famous *The U.S. Field Artillery* march.

The conductor-composer brought his new composition to a resounding close. Breathlessly, the young musicians waited for his reaction. It came in seconds. His face broke into a big grin as he said, "Exactly the way I wanted it to sound."

His remark broke the tension. Each player quickly stood and cheered, stopping only after the bandmaster indicated that he wished to speak.

"Thank you," he said. "You have done an excellent job of sight reading from the manuscript. I am proud of you. The piece will be published exactly as you have played it for me.

"We will play it for the first time in public in the Hippodrome when we go to New York City to assist in both the Liberty Loan and Navy recruiting drives.

"If you will remain standing in your places, I will collect each piece of the manuscript personally." He then moved slowly through the large group of men—a time consuming process—managing in a quiet but friendly manner to communicate in one way or another with each person.

Scores of other interesting and exciting events continued to happen during the remaining months of each enlistee's scheduled training. With few exceptions, the musicians were sent at the end of that period to a ship or other naval installation.

Month after month, Sousa continued to direct the large band. Actually, it was made up of many smaller bands which trained regularly, as companies in a battalion, under chief petty officers. Three of these popular men who whipped such bands into shape were Richard Tainter, head bandmaster, John

Maurice, and Victor J. Grabel.

Sousa and his Recruit Band, as he called it, appeared for concerts, parades, and other ceremonials in Kansas City, Milwaukee, Cleveland, Columbus, Cincinnati, and Pittsburgh.

Also, he took his band to Baltimore, Washington, D.C., Chicago, Philadelphia, and New York City. In the latter city, a spectacular concert was performed in Carnegie Hall. Referring to another performance in New York City, Sousa said later:

> The band gave a concert at the Hippodrome for the Women's Auxiliary Naval Recruiting Station.... For the occasion I wrote the *United States Field Artillery* March and *Blue Ridge*.[22]

Big parades occurred in all of these cities. Regardless of the weather, however, Sousa spurned automobile rides. He chose to march with members of his band.

22. Sousa, *Marching Along*, p. 315.

CHAPTER 14
SOUSA SOLVES ONE OF
THREE PROBLEMS

"I am going to skip the next act," Sousa said to his wife as he excused himself at the intermission and left his box-seat at the theater. He chose to do this occasionally.

Theatergoers that day watched the celebrated musician, spade-beard and all, as he made his way through the crowded lobby. What he did the next hour was publicized all over the country. Friendly editors described it as one of the big events of the war.

Early in his career, Sousa's beard assumed all of the characteristics of a trademark. Now, at sixty-two and in a naval officer's uniform, he faced a different situation.

The great event was about to take place in the theater's barber shop. Sousa entered the shop wearing both the mustache and the carefully trimmed beard. Thirty minutes later, he emerged without the beard.

Returning to the box, he slipped into his seat in the now-darkened theater. Mrs. Sousa objected, however, when this "stranger" affectionately patted her on the knee.

Soon the play ended and the lights came on. Hundreds in the audience who recognized him earlier were mystified by the change.

This popular and friendly entertainer always made good copy for the newspapers. In the next few weeks, this episode made whimsical headlines. One newspaper proclaimed that, "This sacrifice will surely bring the war to an earlier close."

The bandmaster stated to reporters that he simply considered the beard as inappropriate for the leader of a group of young musicians.

One day a few weeks later, Sousa started the rehearsal with: "We will begin playing this overture in our concerts next week in Detroit. Today, we will smooth out some of the rough spots. Let's start by playing the first half well enough to avoid stopping for corrections."

The band got off to a fine start. Within minutes, however, a

45

Sousa shaved off his famous beard in 1918 so he would better fit in with his youthful U.S. Navy musicians. "That won the war," he declared. "Kaiser Bill surrendered, knowing he could not possibly defeat a nation of men who were willing to make such sacrifices."

small group of officers silently entered the rehearsal room through a door ten feet behind the conductor. Newspapers of the day before had reported the visit of a Russian admiral.

Obviously, two young officers were now giving the admiral and his interpreter a tour of the Training Center. The distinguished guest apparently wanted to meet Sousa. The two naval officers became restless as, unobserved by the conductor, the group waited for a break to occur in the overture rehearsal.

Finally, the playing stopped. The group approached the podium whereupon the surprised Sousa and the admiral were introduced. They saluted and shook hands. The clearly pleased admiral said, through the interpreter, that he wished to remain and listen for a few more minutes. This they all did. At a subsequent break, they waved to the stand and left the hall.

During this break, surprisingly, one of the American naval officers returned to the room. Sousa and this officer were both lieutenants. He walked quickly to the podium and said in a voice loud enough for dozens of players to hear, "Lieutenant Sousa, with the position you occupy in the musical world, you will be introduced to hundreds of superior officers. Each time it happens you *must* step down from your platform."

Obviously, no one knew what the talented composer thought. It seemed unbelievable that something like this could happen. With a gesture which seemed to mean, "You can't win them all," he turned back to the overture and continued with the morning's rehearsal.

He must have felt, as did the writer, that even had it been a warranted rebuke, the officer administered it in the poorest possible manner.

In November of that year, a young lieutenant, who was a member of the Band Battalion, called out, "This is Lieutenant Sousa's sixty-third birthday." As Sousa made his way to the podium, the young man continued, "Let's give him a big hand."

The shocked members responded with only polite applause. So he was *sixty-three*. One player, saddened by the

47

disclosure, thought of the conductor as having only a few more years to live. Others must have had similar thoughts.

The bandmaster appeared to be somewhat startled at the lack of enthusiasm. Nonetheless, he felt the need to say something before beginning the day's work. Ordinarily, when he addressed the band, his remarks were casual. They were often witty. This was not one of those occasions. For reasons of his own, he brought his "speech" to a close in about thirty seconds.

Quickly, he turned to the pieces to be rehearsed that day. For the next hour, he drove the band at a pace much harder than usual. Possibly the members of the band had affronted him. At the end of a second hour of vigorous directing and energetic playing, everyone must have forgotten the incident.

All bandmasters know that a large band, made up mostly of amateurs, is likely to seesaw on occasion. Often such a band will also play out of tune. After two hours of rehearsing, this band did both.

Faced with the situation, Sousa, even though noted for his optimism, could have been excused for thinking, "Surely I could have selected a better way to contribute to the war effort."

Regardless of what he was thinking, he stopped the band suddenly. In a slightly exasperated voice, he said something that he had said a dozen times before. Today's birthday episode, however, gave the remark a special significance.

With some sarcasm he called out: "Will you please get together before I die?" Judging by the quick change of expression on Sousa's face, he realized that his words had changed the mood. The young men he faced, were, again, thinking of his extremely advanced age.

CHAPTER 15
AN ABERRATION TRIGGERS
A MAKE-BELIEVE ACT

Sousa brought the medley they were rehearsing to a quick stop. He addressed the members of the twenty-four piece clarinet section. "You are letting the tempo drag for these first few measures of your 'solo.' This *Sailor's Hornpipe* dance movement must start at break-neck speed."

Sousa enjoyed rehearsing this particular medley. It contained a dozen or more tuneful melodies including this spirited dance. The score called for this large clarinet section to play the *Hornpipe* unaccompanied by the band. It was one of the most exciting parts of the entire selection. Subsequently, when played in public, audiences would break into the piece with their applause when this particular movement ended.

This was one of the band's better rehearsals. Nonetheless, an incident soon occurred which all bandmasters have probably witnessed at one or more times in their careers. Everything went along very well from the start of the medley until a point just before the dance movement was to begin. At this stage, the briefest of pauses took place.

Here, the solo clarinetist made an error. Without looking at the bandmaster, he plunged swiftly into the fast-paced dance movement about one-half second before the cue was to have been given. No other clarinetist followed him into this false start.

Surprisingly, Sousa anticipated the miscue by possibly a hundredth of a second. Instantly, he made it clear that the young man was to continue to perform as an individual soloist that he had suddenly made of himself.

An audience, had there been one, would not have known of the aberration. Spectators would have seen a completely poised conductor carefully guiding a musician through a well-rehearsed solo. Playfully, however, the conductor speeded up the tempo. It became an amusing contest which the young clarinetist easily won. Sousa signaled for the band to return to the place where the error occurred and to proceed as if nothing

Sousa led his 300-piece "Recruit" band, or other smaller bands, in many parades during World War I to support Liberty Loan and Red Cross fund drives. This is a May, 1917, parade in Chicago.

had happened.

Something else, however, was taking place. Almost imperceptibly the bandmaster touched his lips to indicate that an audience was present. Thus alerted, the band concentrated on the remainder of the medley as if performing in a completely filled auditorium.

The tolerant drillmaster, now turned entertainer, ended the selection with his characteristic *public* flourish. Also, he gave a friendly nod to the members of the band. These amenities had never before occurred at rehearsals.

Having done this, he stepped down from his podium and walked five feet away from the front row of the band. At that spot, he stopped at the edge of an imaginary stage and, with dignity, bowed to the left, the center, and to the right. As he turned away, he waved his baton in a friendly manner to the non-existent balconies.

After shaking hands with and complimenting the soloist, he motioned for him to go to the front of the "stage" for his "curtain call." With clarinet in hand and with an appropriate show of modesty, the clarinetist made his three bows and returned to his seat.

The poise and skill displayed by the young musician in playing the initial solo under exciting conditions and the manner in which he led the section on the repeating of the movement impressed everyone. Sousa dropped the play-acting role and motioned for the players to applaud.

Few of those present would ever forget the soloist's amusing miscue and the humorous make-believe act it triggered on the part of Sousa.

CHAPTER 16
SOUSA PERFORMING AT HIS BEST

Many times in a single season, with Sousa's cooperation, outstanding concerts were raised to the level of superlative performances.

When he was in his sixties, an example of this occurred. It took place one Saturday afternoon in a large city in one of the finest concert halls in the United States. He followed a long-standing custom. Invariably, he started playing an encore about twenty-seconds after the end of the preceding piece. Audiences would still be applauding.

At this matinee, the conductor responded generously to the call for a highly unusual number of encores during the first half of the program. A sensational performance appeared to be in the making.

With three scheduled pieces still to be played, the audience insisted on five encores end-to-end. When the bandmaster raised his baton to start the next scheduled number, he waited for the applause to stop. A moment of complete silence descended on the darkened concert hall.

Surprisingly, at that precise moment, someone whistled the opening bars of *The Washington Post* march. The sound came from the highest balcony.

An amused murmur rose from the expectant audience. The bandmaster made no change in his posture except for a slight nod to his players. He continued to hold his baton high. Only a few musicians changed music on their stands.

Delaying only these few seconds, Sousa answered the message from the balcony with the strains of that piece he had penned over thirty years earlier.

The audience reacted spontaneously. It broke into a roar of applause. They were delighted with his incredible act of musical showmanship.

These enthusiastic listeners asked for and got a total of over thirty encores that day. All were selections created by Sousa. The listeners insisted that *The Stars and Stripes Forever* be played twice and the part starting with the piccolo obbligato

Shortly after Sousa had been promoted to lieutenant commander in 1919, he autographed this photo for the author.

be repeated two additional times.

This exhilarating performance ended very late that afternoon. There had been many like it. Close friends of Sousa quickly whisked him away for a prearranged party. Backstage, players placed their instruments in cases. Many of the men hurried to the main lobby to wait for friends. The emotionally drained crowd moved slowly through the lobby to the street.

Two young couples, visibly exhausted from their afternoon's experience, stopped in front of one of the waiting musicians. They examined him as if he were a statue. The strange silence ended when one of the women, obviously a musician, recognized the instrument case he carried.

"I, too, play flute and piccolo," she said. Then brightening, she asked, "So you are one of the four who played the obbligato? And we made you play it many times."

"Yes indeed," came the reply.

"How long have you been playing with Sousa?"

"Four months," the young man answered.

"Can you imagine the good fortune," the girl remarked as she turned to leave, "of playing that long with the *greatest entertainer* of all time?"

CHAPTER 17
A RARE PERSONAL MEETING AND
DINNER WITH THE COMPOSER IN 1922

"As you know, Mr. Sousa," the university senior remarked, "there have been several stories in the newspapers recently about your hobbies. Which do you enjoy the most?"

Sousa was visiting with bandmaster A. Austin Harding and five members of the University of Illinois Concert Band. They were entertaining Sousa at dinner prior to the start of his concert. The five young men dining that evening in Champaign, Illinois, were undergraduate officers of the band in 1922.

World War I had ended three years earlier with Sousa having spent almost eighteen months on active duty. During the entire period, he demonstrated his remarkable skill as an executive and his extraordinary ability as a conductor and composer.

Upon leaving the navy, he reconstituted the tours of his civilian band and continued to enhance his worldwide reputation as a conductor and creator of music. The year following his return to civilian life, he was promoted to the rank of lieutenant commander in the U.S. Naval Reserve.

Three of the university band's officers present at the dinner were graduating seniors. One of them had attended the reception at Great Lakes that welcomed Sousa into the U.S. Navy and subsequently played for many months in his Naval Training Station band.

This early evening dinner, which preceded Sousa's civilian band concert, became an unforgettable event.

"Yes, I have read these stories," he replied. "With me, baseball comes first, next is horseback riding, and third is trapshooting. Recent articles have publicized the fact that I am now president of both the American Amateur Trapshooting Association and the National Association of Shotgun Owners." Another short discussion took place about his other hobbies.

Sousa then brought up the subject of his accident. It, too, had been highly publicized by the newspapers. "Actually," he said, "when my horse threw me, the fall broke my back and smashed my left shoulder. It happened last September. I was in great pain. Concerts were canceled while I spent weeks in bed or otherwise out of circulation. Of course, I paid every player's salary during this period while we were all idle. The accident almost ended my career."

Discussing the accident obviously distressed him. One young man, wishing to divert him from the subject, asked, "Mr. Sousa, are you preparing to publish your autobiography?"

"Finally, I can say 'yes.' Reporters ask me that question several times a year," he answered. "The project is now only in its first stage. Although I am enjoying the work, my progress is slow.

"It will appear first as a series of five or six articles published in the *Saturday Evening Post*. At my present rate, it will take eighteen months or more to complete the manuscript. The editors want to call it *Keeping Time*. I would like to give it the title *Men, Women and Music I Have Known*. The year following the magazine articles, the series is scheduled to be published as a book.

"This," he continued, "will be my seventh book, of which three are novels." The seemingly relaxed celebrity visited comfortably with everyone present. Graciously, he said he envied the seniors, all of whom were facing new careers.

The men entertaining Sousa were not unaware of the fact that they were visiting with probably the first serious musician in the world ever to become a millionaire. It was known that he had accomplished this entirely on his own without a subsidy of any kind. They knew also that he was reputed to be a very astute collector.

"We have been told very little about your famous collector's library. We are anxious to know more about it." This was to be the last subject they would discuss.

"It has always been a pleasure to collect books," Sousa answered. "As a boy, I always had a few dozen or more in my room. Now, there are more than 3,000 books and manuscripts

Sousa was a man of many talents, writing prose as well as music. He was the author of seven books, including three novels, and many other literary pieces. He collected rare books and had a sizable personal library.

in what I like to call my private library. By the way, when we were talking about hobbies a few minutes ago, I did not mention my preoccupation with this library. Of course it, too, is a hobby.

"Every time I return from a tour, I spend days reading and examining the new acquisitions. I should say that some of the items were boxed and stored for many years until we bought our first home seven or eight years ago. Until that time, the Sousa family lived in hotels and apartments. Now we all have our beautiful three-acre place at Sands Point, Long Island. It is near Port Washington.

"As to the long-term future of my music library, I expect to donate it to a university or give it to the Library of Congress." With this, he discreetly glanced at his watch.

All of the men walked the four blocks to the Auditorium. At the stage entrance they said their goodbyes to Sousa and, through another door, went to their reserved seats.

Within minutes, Sousa appeared. That night the university community enjoyed the type of concert that only Sousa and his band could perform.

As engrossing as the concert was, however, the mind of one listener wandered momentarily to the earlier conversation about Sousa's books and manuscripts. Just conceivably, this celebrated musician's special library might take its place with many other valuable and outstanding collections at the University of Illinois.

Years later, the first shipment of these treasures did arrive at the University of Illinois. It consisted of forty-two trunks containing the most important part of this great musician's library, his podium, music stand, and many other significant pieces.[23]

The Sousa Band music library and other memorabilia occupies a major section of a museum on the second floor of the Band Department building, now known as the Harding Band Building.

23. Burford, *We're Loyal to You, Illinois*, p. 483.

CHAPTER 18
MEMBERS OF SOUSA'S CIVILIAN BAND ENABLE HIM TO ARRIVE ON TIME

"Marquette University is awarding me the honorary degree of Doctor of Music," said Sousa to William Schneider, the traveling manager of his civilian band.

"Do you have to appear in person to receive it?" asked Schneider.

"Indeed I do. I must be in Milwaukee on the morning of November 26, 1923."

"If we just had airplanes flying between our large cities, there would be no difficulties. As it is, with police escorts helping you at all transfer points, we might make it," commented Schneider. He continued to examine both the schedule of the tour and his books of train arrivals and departures. "However, we are going to have problems."

"The night before the ceremony in Milwaukee," he continued, "we have a concert in Akron, Ohio. Worse still, we give a matinee in Hammond, Indiana, the afternoon of the day of the ceremony."

"At the matinee," Sousa said, "I could pick up a half-hour by starting it with our new *Showing Off Before Company*. As you know, the musicians precede me, in small groups, on the stage." He had created this amusing piece only three years earlier.

"That will probably do it," exclaimed Schneider. "All of us want you to be present to accept this honorary award from Marquette."

The regular tour for the 1923 season started on schedule. On a night, several weeks later and only minutes after the end of the concert in Akron, Schneider rushed Sousa to the railroad station. He said goodbye to him as he placed him on the midnight train for Chicago. Upon arriving there, he transferred to the Chicago, North Shore and Milwaukee Electric Railroad for the final ninety miles.

Good natured police escorts, notified in advance, aided him at every possible point. In Milwaukee, they hurriedly

Courtesy Paul E. Bierley

One of Sousa's honorary doctorates was awarded by Marquette University in 1923. Attending the morning ceremony called for split-second timing, because the band had an evening concert in Akron the night before and a matinee on the day of the ceremony in Hammond, Indiana.

whisked him to the ceremony with more than a half hour to spare.

The Marquette University officials understood the band-master's urgent problem. Known for the smooth manner in which they conducted their ceremonies, the officials immediately conferred the degree on the "Great American Composer and Conductor." In a very short time, Sousa found himself free to leave the university and its huge crowd of well-wishers.

The return trip became an exciting race.

Police escorts and others did everything they could. With all of this help, the bandmaster made it only to the outskirts of the city of Hammond by starting time for the concert. Individual members would now be appearing on the stage to amuse the audience with their special musical presentations.

You have probably guessed it. Sousa made his entrance on the stage in an unhurried manner. The Hammond audience did not have the slightest idea that the sirens they heard outside were bringing the conductor of the concert that had already started.

CHAPTER 19
ACTIVITIES FROM 1925 TO 1932

By 1925, Sousa had directed continuously one or the other of his three famous bands for forty-five years. As previously recounted, he became leader of the United States Marine Band in 1880; formed his own professional civilian band in 1892 and continued with it until suspending its activities in 1917. For the next eighteen months, Sousa organized and directed the United States Naval Training Station Band. Finally, he regrouped his civilian band in 1919 and returned to the more traditional schedule of engagements and tours of the pre-1917 period.

By 1921, many younger musicians—such as Meredith Willson—were employed. Many other talented young men— Edwin E. Newcomb, Richard (Dick) Kent, and Arthur Nelson Brabrook from the 1921 and 1922 University of Illinois Bands—joined this famous professional touring concert band.

Although no additional European tours were attempted, the band crisscrossed the United States each year of the 1920's and in 1930 and 1931.

Sousa and the band played regular engagements at Philadelphia's Willow Grove Park until 1926. Then a series started at Atlantic City's Steel Pier. Among other things, the band played a very successful engagement at the 1926 Cleveland Exposition and at numerous state fairs.

With gentle but persistent urging, the editors of the *Saturday Evening Post* persuaded Sousa to complete the manuscript of the story of his life. It was published in six of the weekly issues between October and December, 1925. Also, but not quite on schedule, the same materials, updated and augmented, appeared as a book in 1928.

In 1929, the band's first radio broadcasts were made for General Motors on the WEAF network of the National Broadcasting Co.

Fortunately for the younger generation, Sousa became especially interested in high school band development.

Sousa had great faith in the future of American music and enthusiastically supported the school music movement. He is shown here at the
National Music Camp in Interlochen, Michigan, with Joseph Maddy,
president of the camp (left) and A. Austin Harding, bandmaster at the
University of Illinois (right). *The Northern Pines* march (1931) was dedicated to Maddy and the camp.

Courtesy U.S. Marine Band

Sousa and his band performed many times in the New York Hippodrome. For a memorable concert there on November 5, 1922, the band premiered his new march, *The Gallant Seventh*, dedicated to Major Francis Sutherland and the 7th Regiment, 107th Infantry, of the New York National Guard. Sutherland had been a cornetist with Sousa and was the first Sousa bandsman to enlist in the U.S. Army during World War I. The 7th Regiment band is seen behind Sousa's.

Among many other activities in this connection, he acted as guest conductor at the National High School Orchestra and Band Camp at Interlochen, Michigan, in 1930 and 1931. He composed a march for and dedicated it to the camp and donated the royalties to its scholarship fund.[24]

The decade of the 1920's, and the years 1930 and 1931 continued to be great years for the now venerable Sousa. He produced a steady flow of marches. His band was enthusiastically received, and the story of his life was enjoyed by millions of his followers who read either the serialized articles or his book, *Marching Along* (subtitled *Recollections of Men, Women and Music*).

24. Bierley, *The Works of John Philip Sousa*, p. 75.

CHAPTER 20
SOUSA ON RETIREMENT

Sousa maintained a very friendly attitude toward newspaper reporters. Many were close friends. This became evident at the time he left the U.S. Navy in 1918 when he was a little over sixty-three.

"I would like to be a ticket scalper and make a lot of money out of it," one reporter said, "when you give your big farewell concert, Mr. Sousa." In the following years, the question came up regularly as to when he would retire. In all cases, he said there would never be such a concert.

Often he added, "If you hear that I have retired, you will know that I have died."

This man, who had been an international celebrity for many decades, presumably did not want to retire. If true, he certainly got his wish.

What proved to be his final tour with the band ended in September, 1931. In the next five busy months, he completed work on several new marches. Among many other activities, he attended the enormous celebration of his seventy-seventh birthday in November of 1931. Months later, he spent the morning of March 5, 1932, in Philadelphia and the afternoon in Reading, Pennsylvania. He rehearsed the Ringgold Band in Reading and was to be their guest conductor the following day.

After completing a sixteen-hour schedule of activities, including an evening dinner and ceremonial, he returned to his hotel and retired.

John Philip Sousa, who had already become an American institution, died shortly after midnight on March 6, 1932, in his room at the Abraham Lincoln Hotel in Reading.

In the following months, the editors of newspapers and magazines, as well as radio broadcasters, did their utmost to honor a great American. Unquestionably, he would always occupy a position of prestige in the folklore of his country. All agreed that an era had ended. Mrs. Sousa died twelve years later.

Among the millions of words written about Sousa in recent

years are tributes such as these:

More than builders of empires, more than presidents and statesmen, John Philip Sousa illustrates the spirit that is America's. He made that spirit breathe, made it throb in the hearts of generations of Americans with the martial strains of his music.[25]

His life was full-flavored with incident and anecdote, with mellow humor and kindly wisdom. By using well the genius entrusted to him by his Creator, he won success and happiness in advancing one of the finer qualities of human nature—the love of music.[26]

Sixty years after his death, those who played in or heard his concerts may be pardoned if they consider Sousa the greatest entertainer of all time.

25. *Overture*, December, 1953, p. 18.
26. Berger, *The March King and His Band*, p. 62.

BIBLIOGRAPHY
(Quotes used with permission)

BOOKS

Berger, Kenneth. *The March King and His Band*. New York: Exposition Press, 1957.

Bierley, Paul E. *John Philip Sousa, American Phenomenon* (Revised edition). Westerville, Ohio: Integrity Press, 1986.

Bierley, Paul E. *The Works of John Philip Sousa*. Westerville, Ohio: Integrity Press, 1984.

Burford, Cary Clive. *We're Loyal to You, Illinois*. Danville, Illinois: The Interstate, 1952.

Elston, Louis C. *The History of American Music*. New York: Macmillan, 1904.

Lingg, Ann M. *John Philip Sousa*. New York: Henry Holt and Company, 1954.

Sousa, John Philip. *Marching Along*. Boston: Hale, Cushman & Flint, 1928.

ARTICLES

Jones, Stewart and Campbell, William III. "The President's Music Men." *National Geographic Magazine*, December, 1959.

Sousa, John Philip. "Here's Sousa's First Self-Written Interview." *Los Angeles Times* (The Pink Sheet), October 16, 1911.

Sousa, John Philip. "Keeping Time." *The Saturday Evening Post*, October 31, November 7, 21, 28, December 5, 12, 1925 (six articles).

"Sousa Alumni." *Overture* [periodical of the Musicians Mutual Protective Association, Local 47, American Federation of Musicians, Los Angeles, California], December, 1954.

"Sousa Now in the Navy." *Great Lakes Naval Review*, Great Lakes, Illinois, June, 1917."

ABOUT THE AUTHOR

Malcolm Heslip, a graduate of the Mt. Vernon, Illinois, High School, is a retired member of the faculty of the University of California, Los Angeles. In 1919, he left the United States Navy after twenty-seven months of service. This period included the time spent in John Philip Sousa's naval band and the bands at both the U.S. Navy Station at Guantanamo, Cuba, and on the cruiser *USS Columbia*.

After graduating from the University of Illinois and being involved in business in the Chicago area, he changed to a teaching career and returned to the University of Illinois to complete his Ph.D. degree in Economics.

Heslip reestablished his association with the U.S. Navy, however, and received a lieutenant's commission in the Naval Reserve. Following this, during summer vacations, he took many cruises on ships and tours of duty ashore. In 1940, he was promoted to lieutenant commander and ordered to active duty.

During the next five and one-half years, among other things, he graduated from the Naval War College and carried out both temporary and active assignments in North Africa, the Middle East, aboard the *USS Tasker H. Bliss* in the Mediterranean, and with the Navy Department in Washington,

Photograph by Christopher Thompson

The author played this piccolo (left) in Sousa's United States Naval Training Station Band in 1917. The flute (right) was purchased many years later.

D.C. Later, he served as a staff department head at sea in the Seventh Fleet in the Pacific Theater. Promotion to captain came shortly before World War II ended.

Leaving the U.S. Navy again in 1946, he returned to academic life as an assistant professor at the University of Southern California, from which he had been on wartime leave. Within a year, however, he moved to UCLA's Graduate School of Management where he remained as a lecturer and administrator for almost two decades.

Dr. Heslip now lives with his wife Doris in Laguna Hills, California.

INDEX

Abraham Lincoln Hotel, 66
Akron, Ohio, 59, 60
Alexandria Hotel, 36
Amateur Opera Company, 6n
American Amateur Trapshooting
  Association, 55
Arthur, President Chester A., 1, 2, 4, 9
Atlantic City, New Jersey, 62

Baltimore, Maryland, 44
Band Battalion, 47
Bavaria, 2
Bellis, Jane Van Middlesworth, 2, 3, 6,
  7, 8, 8n; *see also* Sousa, Mrs. John
  Philip
Benkert, George Felix, 3
Berger, Kenneth, 14n, 67n
Berlin, Germany, 32, 34
Bierley, Paul E. 2n, 5n, 7, 13, 16, 23n,
  57, 60, 65n
Blakely, David, 12, 17
Blue Ridge, 44
Brabrook, Arthur Nelson, 62
British Cunard *Lusitania*, 39, 39n
Broadway, 6
Brooklyn, New York, 2
Brussels, Belgium, 32, 34
Burford, Cary Clive, 58n

"Cachuca", 1
Cape May, New Jersey, 10
Capitol Building, 9
Carnegie Hall, 44
Carpenter, John Alden, 40
Centennial Orchestra, 3
Champaign, Illinois, 55
Chicago, Illinois, 40, 44, 50, 59
Chicago World's Fair, 12
Cincinnati, Ohio, 44
Civil War, 2
Clarke, Herbert L., 12, 40, 41
Cleveland, Ohio, 44
Cleveland, President Grover, 4, 9
Cleveland Exposition, 62
Columbia Phonograph Company, 9
Columbus, Ohio, 44
Congress, 40
Corn Palace Exposition, 36
Countess of Warwick, 24

Detroit, Michigan, 45
Dillingham, Charles, 37

Drill Hall, 29

Earl of Warwick, 24
Elston, Louis C., 13, 13n
England, 13, 21, 22, 24, 30
Europe, 12, 17, 22, 24, 27, 34, 36, 37,
  62

Fairest of the Fair, The, 29
France, 13
Furrer, Barry Owen, 30

Gallant Seventh, The, 64
Garfield, President James A., 4, 9
General Motors, 62
Georgetown [Washington, D.C.], 3
Germany, 13, 27, 28, 32
Gilbert, William, 6
Gilmore, Patrick S., 12
Glasgow International Exhibition, 36
Gorman's Original Church Choir
  "Pinafore" Company, 6n
Grabel, Victor J., 44
Great Lakes, Illinois, 40
Great Lakes Naval Training Station
  [Center], 40, 42, 47, 55
Great Lakes Naval Training Station
  Band, 40, 41, 43, 44, 45, 47, 48, 49,
  50, 51, 52, 54, 55, 62, 65
Grenadier Guards Band, 22

H.M.S. Pinafore, 6, 6n
Halle, Germany, 34
Hammond, Indiana, 59, 60, 61
Hanover, Germany, 32, 33, 34
Harding, A. Austin, 55, 63
Harding Band Building, 58
Harrison, President Benjamin, 4, 9
Hayes, President Rutherford B., 4, 9
Heidelberg, Germany, 27
Hip Hip Hooray, 37
History of American Music, 13

Illinois, 55
Imperial Edward, 23
Interlochen, Michigan, 63, 65
Interlochen Arts Academy, 63
Italy, 17

John Philip Sousa, 21n
*John Philip Sousa, American
  Phenomenon*, 2n

73